Heal
Your Heartache

Heal
Your Heartache

5 Steps to Reclaim Your Life
After a Breakup, Divorce,
or Loss of a Partner

Deborah Paiva

Red Coral Publishing
DELRAY BEACH, FL

Disclaimer: The information in this book is based upon the personal and professional experiences of the author. It is intended for life-empowerment purposes. It is not intended as a substitute for consulting with a healthcare professional. Any attempt to diagnose and treat an illness or mental health issue should be done under the direction of a healthcare professional. The publisher and author are not responsible for any adverse effects or consequences resulting from the use of the suggestions discussed in this book. Should the reader have any questions concerning the appropriateness of any suggestion mentioned, the author and the publisher strongly suggest consulting a professional healthcare advisor.

Published by

Red Coral Publishing

DELRAY BEACH, FL

www.RedCoralPublishing.com

Library of Congress Control Number: 2018939441

ISBN: 978-1-7321691-0-4

Printed in the United States of America

Cover artwork by Evelyn Stern Ballin at
    http://www.etsy.com/shop/TheHeartPainter
Cover design by Alisha Paiva
Interior layout by Gary A. Rosenberg
Copyedited by Carol Killman Rosenberg

To my clients, past and present.
You inspire me every day
with your courage and your trust.
I am a better coach
and a better person because of you.

Lokah Samastah Sukhino Bhavantu

May all beings everywhere be happy and free,
and may the thoughts, words, and actions
of my own life contribute in some way to
that happiness and to that freedom for all.

Contents

Introduction . . . 1

1
A New Beginning . . . 5

2
The H-E-A-R-T Process . . . 15

STEP 1 Honor Your Feelings . . . 21

STEP 2 Examine Your Beliefs . . . 35

STEP 3 Accept Your Present . . . 53

STEP 4 Release Your Past . . . 63

STEP 5 Transform Your Thoughts
        to Transform Your Life . . . 77

3
Living in New Awareness . . . 89

Acknowledgments . . . 101

About the Author . . . 103

A Gift for You . . . 105

Introduction

Whenever anything difficult happened in my grandmother's life, or in mine, she would always say, "Well that will make a good story." Although I may not have felt exactly that way as I was going through my divorce, I nonetheless knew that it would become part of my story, just as the death of my first husband had.

Our lives are like a tapestry, with everything we experience woven in and creating all of the textures and colors of who we become. The death of my first husband, David, was a big part of my tapestry. It didn't matter that we'd been married for fewer than three years, had lived together for even less time than that, or had struggled to define our relationship in terms that were comfortable for each of us. None of that mattered. All that mattered was that he was my first love and now he was gone. I was a widow. I struggled with depression and remorse. It became part of my inner being for more years than I realized, even through my next marriage. I clung so tightly to my second husband, Ken, for fear of that abandonment again, but after many years together, I finally relaxed into the comfort and the love we had for each other.

Unfortunately, nothing in this life is ever truly under our control, other than our own attitude. Our beautiful marriage suddenly began to unravel, and I tried desperately to save it. In the end I had no choice but to let it go. I cried every day for a year and a half, while wondering if I'd ever be able to stop. Yet even through those tears I had a glimpse of a new purpose in my life. It was as if additional textures were being woven into my life's tapestry at that very moment. I grew more and more determined to find a way out, a way to the other side, to freedom and joy again. I couldn't see it at the time, but I did remember what it felt like to be happy, and that memory created a little spark, like a light in the darkness that I clung to. I followed that tiny spark through a maze of healing. I read, I prayed, I journaled, I tried to meditate, I cried, and I got angry, mostly at myself for being so lost. I was depressed, but I was determined to survive. I succumbed to fear at times, and I fought to stay whole at other times. I mourned the loss of my relationship. It was the "we" that I grieved, the "us" that I missed. Yet through all the sadness and occasional fits of anger, I kept following that flicker of hope, like a lit candle leading me through the darkness, and I knew that if I could survive, I could help others to as well.

I'd like to tell you that I was good at this healing thing, but it was a terribly messy process for me. I didn't always follow my own intuitive guidance. I often fought it, and I sabotaged myself. However, when my sadness overcame my body, it created a major health crisis in my life, and I finally had to dig deep to find the warrior within. I became that warrior, and through my healing journey, I found my way back to light and joy, and I reclaimed my life. I'm not saying that it was easy, but I am saying that it was worth it. Someone I met at a support meeting once told me that my life would never be the same again. That tore me apart because I wanted my beautiful life back and I wanted my husband back. But the truth is that my life wasn't perfect back then. It was good, but there were also situations in my life that I was choosing to ignore, and when we aren't totally present and facing our fears, things often fall apart.

I can now say that I truly love my life and the person I've become. I even love my ex-husband more because I see him more clearly, in his honest humanness, and that's a true blessing to us both.

So, this book is the result of my healing process. My purpose in writing it is to help you begin to heal your sadness, anger, or fear before it overtakes your body, steals your peace of mind, and affects your health. I've walked the road you're on. I know the way, and I've done the healing. I don't have all the answers, certainly not for your life and not even for mine. However, I know the path, and I'd like to offer you some hope along the way. You can find a release from the sadness, anger, or fear that has invaded your life, and you can heal your heartache. There is a way out of the darkness if you're willing to keep moving forward.

This little book is meant to be a beginning to deeper self-discovery. It's a guide through a process of healing that can take you as deep as you desire to go. Don't be afraid. Just open your heart a bit and let the light in as we take the steps together. I hope you discover a gift within these pages. Perhaps it will be the knowledge that you aren't alone in your pain, the glimmer of hope that you can find your way to joy again, or perhaps simply the gift of understanding yourself or another a little more. I believe that if you open your heart just a bit, you'll feel mine in these pages. This is a gift from my heart to yours.

1

A New Beginning

Losing a partner through death, divorce, or a breakup is the hardest thing that most of us will ever have to bear. We've all heard the statement "Everything happens for a reason," which often can make us feel like screaming. Yet as hard as it is to deal with loss, and it can be gut-wrenching as we know, there is an amazing blessing on the other side of it. Heartache brings us to our knees. However, if we don't succumb to the depression, and we take whatever steps we can to move forward, no matter how small, we can get to a place where we are in awe of our own resilience. It's that resilience that becomes the lifeline to our empowerment.

I have met a number of people who have been widowed, betrayed, or abandoned and never moved on from that sad place. I was determined that would not be my story. I had been told by a friend that it would be hard for me to open my heart again and to ever trust again. I remember thinking that she was so wrong and that I would never allow this experience to define me. The truth is that the way people think about us, or even treat us, really has nothing to do with us. It has everything to do with them, their own fears, their own beliefs, and their own insecurities. It serves us well to remember that and helps us remain true to who we are. We are unique, not a copy, nor are we a blueprint of what someone else expects us to be. We cannot let our losses define us.

I was a student, then I was a wife, then I was a young widow, then I was a wife (for a very long time), and then I was a divorcee. Yet that's not who I am. None of that defines me. They were simply roles I took on, along with the role of daughter, sister, niece, stepmother, godmother, aunt, friend, vocalist, coach, speaker, and author. I have embraced all of those roles. However, they do not define me because I am so much more than how the world sees me. I am, in varying degrees at times, a powerful, loving, intuitive, loyal, creative, and spiritual woman. That is how I choose to define myself.

So how have you been defining yourself? Have you been allowing others to define you or tell you how you should be feeling or behaving? If so stop now! This is *your* glorious life. Even if it hasn't seemed so glorious lately, it can be all that and so much more. The bad news is that it's totally up to you, and the good news is that it's totally up to you! You are in the driver's seat. You can make all the decisions for your life. The choices are all yours. You can choose to stay stuck in sadness, anger, or fear or you can choose to move on and create a life that inspires and excites you. If this seems too mind-boggling or overwhelming right now, don't fret. The process isn't complicated, and you have the right to move at your own pace. Remember this is not a race; it's your life.

At this point, before you go any further, take a moment to pause and reflect on these questions:

1. Do you feel content in your life right now, or do you feel that something is missing?

   _____

   _____

   _____

2. Do you feel a sense of overall happiness, or do you experience moments of sadness, anger, or fear about the past or about the future?

   _____

   _____

   _____

3. Do you feel empowered to move forward, or are you feeling stuck?

   _____

   _____

   _____

If you aren't as content as you'd like to be or if you'd like to feel happier and more empowered, then you're in the right place. Other people have survived the loss of a partner and moved on. Many have even found love again. All of that is possible. So, if any of that is what you want, then make a commitment to yourself to keep an open mind as we continue.

The sad truth is that many people will choose to stay exactly where they are even if they are in pain from intense anger or sadness. We can get accustomed to anything if we stay in one place long enough. It becomes our comfort zone, even as we complain about how uncomfortable we are. It's part of the enigma of being human. We can wallow in our own misery and blame life or God or other humans for the way we feel, but the fact is that no one can make us feel anything. We have free will, and we have the power to choose how we respond to each and every situation that occurs in our life.

Life takes courage, and it's not easy to feel courageous when everything we planned and believed about our lives has turned upside down. When I was younger, I used to think that I had courage; however, upon reflection I see that I was indeed daring and impulsive, but that's not courage. Courage is a willingness to step away from what's comfortable, stand in our own integrity, and speak our truth with compassion. It's being able to face the fear and not allow it to paralyze us, but to use it to spur us on to a greater purpose. Courage is a muscle we have to keep flexing. It takes courage to admit that we're scared sometimes or that we don't know what to do next. Yet so many others are feeling the same way, and when we admit to our fears, we give others the courage to admit to theirs too. We then begin to realize that we aren't alone.

Although you may often feel that you're walking this healing journey alone, I promise you that you have company, support, and understanding. There is so much light on the other side of this process. Taking one step can make such a difference in your life. You really have nothing to lose by moving forward and you have so much to gain.

2

The H-E-A-R-T
Process

*"Life shrinks or expands
in proportion to one's courage."*

—Anais Nin

STEP 1 **H**onor Your Feelings

STEP 2 **E**xamine Your Beliefs

STEP 3 **A**ccept Your Present

STEP 4 **R**elease Your Past

STEP 5 **T**ransform Your Thoughts
to Transform Your Life

STEP 1

Honor Your Feelings

You have the right to feel whatever it is you're feeling right now. If you're sad or you're angry or you're fearful, you have the right to feel this way. You've had a great loss in your life and everything has shifted, so emotions shift as well. Be compassionate with yourself, and remember that you are grieving. Even if it seems as though it's taking a long time to feel better, it's okay because everyone grieves differently. You're not on a time clock. Remember, you don't have to follow anyone else's blueprint for your life. This is your life, so all decisions and choices are yours to make.

Your Pain Is Not Just Emotional, It Is Physical as Well

I've always had a strong and independent spirit, so I assumed that I could get through anything, but at age twenty-one, the death of my first husband shook me to my core. I blamed myself for everything: our relationship issues, his health, and his behaviors. However, the truth is that it was his life to live the way he wanted to, and he always made his own choices. My choices were all I was responsible for. Yet I was so young and so inexperienced in handling trauma that I became clinically depressed and then suicidal.

At that time, I didn't realize that my pain was physical as well as emotional. I didn't realize this fact until many years later, during the process of divorce with my second husband, when I began feeling those same frightening emotions again. This time I refused to ride the roller coaster of depression without reaching out for help. I'm a voracious reader, so I began reading everything I could to understand what was happening in my heart and in my body. That's when I stumbled upon Dr. Helen Fisher's work, and it became a turning point for me.

Dr. Helen Fisher is an anthropologist who, along with her colleagues Arthur Aron and Lucy Brown, used functional magnetic resonance imaging (fMRI) to study the brain scans of college students who were happily in love and later included people who were suffering from a breakup.

In the first part of the study, they had students who were in love lie in a brain-imaging machine while looking at photos of their love partners and thinking about that person. However, when they were later asked to look at photos of other acquaintances, the students had trouble shifting their focus away from their love partner. They just couldn't stop thinking about the person they loved. The researchers spent several months trying to find ways to help the students stop thinking about their partners during the imaging, but to no avail. It showed them what a powerful force romantic love is.[1]

Their research specifically showed that when a person is thinking about a romantic partner, the dopamine-rich areas of the brain light up. Those dopamine-rich regions, such as the ventral tegmental area (VTA), are known as the motivation and reward system of the brain, and they're activated when we satisfy a deep hunger or thirst, receive a message or call from a love partner, and ingest cocaine. The fact that romantic love reacts in our brain in much the same way as thirst, hunger, or a drug led the researchers to conclude that romantic love is more of a drive than

---

1. Fisher, Aron, et al., "Romantic Love: an fMRI Study of a Neural Mechanism for Mate Choice," *The Journal of Comparative Neurology* 493:58–62 (2005); Aron, Fisher, et al., "Reward, Motivation, and Emotion Systems Associated With Early-Stage Intense Romantic Love," *Journal of Neurophysiology,* Vol. 94, No. 1, pages 327–337 (2005).

an emotion. This can be supported by the fact that when people are in love, they may also be experiencing feelings of anxiousness, anger or sadness, and intense cravings for their partner when they aren't with them.

In further studies with people who had experienced a breakup, they found that the craving for their past partner was as strong as hunger, thirst, or an addiction to cocaine, and just as hard to break away from. Dr. Fisher compares romantic love to a wonderful addiction when all is going well, and a horrible one when the relationship goes wrong.

I remember the very first time I heard Dr. Fisher speak. It immediately changed the way I thought about myself. Up until then the sadness that I was feeling as a result of my divorce was so overwhelming. It came in waves that rushed over me when I least expected it. I felt like a weak and powerless woman. I began to think that I was emotionally unstable, and it frightened me. I couldn't seem to get a grip on myself. However, Dr. Fisher's study and the conclusions she drew made me realize that the pain I was feeling was real and also physical, not just emotional. It made me understand that I wasn't weak or helpless; I was simply going through a natural withdrawal process. I was grieving the loss of romantic love in my life, and I was not crazy—I was simply in pain. I needed to know that, and even though it didn't immediately take the pain away, it did give me an incredible sense of relief and also a sense of hope that I could get through this.

Face the Pain Head On

Facing our feelings isn't easy, but the truth is that if we don't face them, the emotional pain will remain within us and come out in ways we can't possibly predict. Sometimes our emotional pain comes out in conversations when we explode at someone, and we don't even know what happened. Other times it comes out in our bodies. Our bodies can't hold all of the sadness, anger, and fear indefinitely. As our stress level rises, our immune system becomes more compromised and we become more susceptible to disease.

I have a dear friend who, many years ago, was deserted very suddenly by her husband, leaving her with their two young children. She had no idea where he had gone; he had simply packed up his belongings and left. She had no message, no call, and no contact with him for weeks and neither did their children. Her first and only thought was to take care of the children, so she immediately contacted a therapist and made sure that they had the help of a professional to get through this trauma. I applauded her decision and her strong motherly instincts; however, I encouraged her to seek the help of a professional for herself as well. She told me that she was fine as long as her children were taken care of.

I worried about her and what the effects of holding in this emotion while being strong for her children would do to her body. Months after her heart-wrenching divorce, she called to tell me that it had taken her two hours to get from her bed to the bathroom one morning. She said that she woke up and none of her limbs felt functional, and she was in a panic. She explained that she had to slither off the bed, fall to the floor, and literally drag herself to the bathroom and then finally to her phone to call her doctor. Ultimately, she was diagnosed with rheumatoid arthritis and fibromyalgia.

Did the traditional medical professionals tell her that this was possibly an effect of all the anger, sadness, and fear she'd been holding in her body? Absolutely not. They couldn't figure out why someone who was so healthy would "suddenly" come down with these conditions. Interestingly enough her health began to improve many months later when she began facing her emotions. Today, years later, she is practically symptom-free. However, the physical suffering she endured for a number of months almost debilitated her.

So how can you guarantee that your emotions won't cause disease in your body? You can't guarantee that, of course, but you can certainly give yourself the best chance of a healthy survival by releasing your emotions, and there are many ways to do that. Here are a few of them:

Seek the Help of a Professional

Having someone objective to talk to about your loss will give you the permission to speak out loud all the fears you're holding on to so tightly. It will free you from stuffing all that sadness and anger down and give you the license to express it in a safe and nonjudgmental environment, with someone who is trained in asking the right questions to help you go deep into that dark place, while still feeling safe and supported. I can't stress enough how important it is to your healing process to have the level of support and encouragement that a professional has been trained to provide.

Talk Often to a Positive, Encouraging, and Supportive Friend

I initially sabotaged my own healing when I was going through my divorce by abandoning my own meditation practice, the meditation classes and other workshops I had been teaching, and even the amazing books I had always read and recommended. Many of those things had been a support system for me, as they were for my clients, but my sadness had taken over and I began hiding out alone at home more often. In retrospect, I believe that I felt like a fraud, as if my first husband's death was somehow my failure, and now my long-term marriage falling apart was also my failure. The blessing was that I opened up to two very special women who understood my pain. My dear friends Karin and Elizabeth both held the space for me to be sad, without judgment, and they became my lifeline back to sanity. I will forever be grateful.

Please be sure to choose, very wisely, the friend or friends you speak to, as not everyone is able to be there for us in the way we need someone to be. I have people in my life who seemed to take my marriage falling apart, and even myself falling apart, very personally, as if it were too painful for them to handle and they just wanted me to feel better and move on. Those are not the people who can help you now. They have their own timetable in mind, not yours. Remember, your life is not a blueprint of someone else expectations; it's about you honoring your own process.

Also be aware that even your dearest friends may not be available to you now. I had a best friend from college who was there for me when my first husband died.

She was my rock. For years we were there for each other through all of our life experiences, including her two marriages, two children, and two divorces, as well as my second marriage and my experience in becoming a step-mother. However, when my divorce happened she wasn't able to be there for me. She had divorced five years earlier, and she was still grieving.

I felt hurt at first, but as I grew in my awareness of my own healing process, I came to realize I had two amazing friends who were there for me, and it wasn't her job to be one of them. She wasn't emotionally available at that time, and that was okay. I love her, and she continues to be one of my dearest friends. At some point in my life, I also may have been unavailable to a friend in need when I wasn't in a solid emotional place, and I can only hope they understood that as well. So choose the friends you rely on wisely, and be sure that they are nonjudgmental and have the emotional strength you need at this time. You'll know who they are because they'll declare themselves as that person by calling often to check on you while honoring your feelings and your space.

Journal Your Feelings

This is such a powerful way to release your emotions, and it's the practice that helped me the most after the sudden death of my first husband. Years later it was journaling that once again helped me through a divorce I never saw coming. We can't always express our darkest thoughts to others. Sometimes we just can't bear to hear them spoken out loud. It isn't always easy to write those thoughts down either, but it's so important to release them from those dark spaces in our minds, and journaling does that. It helps us to release the negative emotions from our bodies so we can breathe more comfortably again.

To help you get started, I'd like you to reflect on and answer the following questions. You can use the lines below each question to write out your answers or use a journal, a notebook, or the note pages provided in the back of this book. This can be a very powerful process if you allow it to be. I truly believe that we have the ability to heal our heartache. I have proved that in my own life, and I have seen it happen with many of my friends and clients as well. However, it does take some work. This isn't always an easy process, but if you take this time for reflection you can begin to find relief. This process will help you to release those feelings that are bottled up inside of you causing you pain. There is no right or wrong answer to any of these questions. This is simply about you honoring who you are and being as honest with yourself as possible.

A Journaling Exercise

1. What are you struggling with right now?

_____

_____

_____

2. Are you sad? Why or why not?

_____

_____

_____

3. Are you angry? Why or why not?

_____

_____

_____

4. What is the hardest part of this process for you?

_____

_____

_____

5. What would you like to happen next?

_____

_____

_____

6. If that were to happen, would it help you feel more positive about yourself and your future?

_____

_____

_____

7. Is there any way you can begin to see this process in a more positive way?

_____

_____

_____

8. How would you like your future to look?

_____

_____

_____

9. What would you like to create in your life as you move forward?

_____

_____

_____

10. What do you feel you need to have in your life in order to feel better?

_____

_____

_____

11. What is one thing you could do for yourself to feel a bit better right now?

_____

_____

_____

12. What is one step you could take to help yourself feel more positive about your life and your future?

_____

_____

I'm asking you to honor your feelings by facing the pain head-on. Any of the previous methods will work, or better yet use them all. The more you can release your thoughts and emotions, the less bottled up they'll be and the less likely they'll be to hide in the darkness where they can't be healed. Your thoughts need to be spoken or written for their power over you to dissipate. So bring them out and shine the light on them. I know this takes courage, but remember that the more you flex that muscle, the stronger you'll become.

STEP 2

Examine Your Beliefs

As we grow up we accumulate certain beliefs. We may assume they came from our own thought process. The truth is, however, that our oldest beliefs are inherited or adapted from our parents, our teachers, our religious training, and even our friends. These inherited beliefs are so deeply ingrained because we learned them as children and we've thought them and repeated them so often that they have created deeply embedded neural pathways in our brains. A neural pathway is like a superhighway of nerve cells that transmits messages. As we travel that same superhighway with our thoughts and behaviors over and over again, the path becomes very solid and familiar. So we have, in essence, created habits of programmed responses to certain stimuli.

I often explain neural pathways to my clients this way: Imagine that we have rented a cottage by a lake. Between our lovely cottage and the lake, there are high weeds growing. The first time we head to the lake we have to make a conscious decision on how to get through those weeds. So, if there is no path yet, we'll decide where to start walking, and we'll then flatten out some of those weeds with our feet as we walk through them. The second time we head to the lake we'll find that we automatically take the same path, as it's already been flattened, so it's easier this time.

Each time we now head to the lake we take exactly the same path through the weeds without even thinking about it. It just makes sense. It's comfortable to take the path that's already been cleared, so it becomes a programmed response. In this same way, we create neural pathways in our brains by having the same response over and over to the same stimulus. We don't stop to question why because that programmed response just seems correct, when actually it has just become comfortable and familiar.

So how does this relate to your pain? Well, ask yourself: what responses are you having to the story that is going on in your life right now or to the loss you've suffered? What beliefs about love, marriage, or relationships are you still holding on to? Is it a belief that says true love never dies or that marriage is forever? Is it a belief that says when you love someone you must be loyal no matter what they do? Is it a belief that says you are responsible for everything that happens in your life and that you are to blame if a relationship doesn't work out? Is it a belief that says that if someone leaves you, whether from death, abandonment, or betrayal, that it must be your fault or that you didn't do enough or that you somehow don't deserve happiness? Is it a belief that says there is only one true love for each of us and that was your one shot? Is it a belief that says you must remain married no matter what happens or that if you do divorce you may never marry again? Unfortunately, many of those beliefs were my own.

We have held these beliefs for so long that to us they feel like the truth when they may in fact simply be inherited family teachings passed down through generations. We fail to ask ourselves if this long-held belief is what we truly feel in our own hearts. Do we really believe that we are meant to be alone, even if we have been betrayed or abandoned, have an unhappy marriage, or have become widowed? The point I'm trying to make is that you are free to believe anything you like, but be certain that it's your own. If not, then this may be the time to release beliefs that no longer serve you. This is your choice because this is your life.

To help clarify, let me interject a bit of my own experience. When I married my first husband, we were deeply in love and we just wanted to be together. However, I never really wanted to be married. I just wanted to live with him and experience life with him. I wasn't all that interested in the ring, the dress, or the wedding; in fact, the title of "wife" wasn't at all comfortable to me. I didn't want to be a wife, I wanted to simply be Deborah, and I wanted to be with David. I know that David felt exactly the same way. However, we were living in a time and place where that was impossible. I was only nineteen and he was twenty-two, and marriage was the only option we had to live together given the beliefs our families held. So we decided to get married. I certainly never voiced my opinion about wanting to live with David. Instead, we made the valiant effort of convincing our parents, and even ourselves, that we were ready, and we eventually got caught up in the excitement of it all. However, my fears about marriage never went away, even as I walked down the aisle with my dad at my side. I didn't have the courage to speak up and stand in my own truth.

I had no doubt of my love for David or his love for me, but as we know love isn't the only ingredient needed to make a marriage work. Marriage takes a different kind of commitment and a maturity that neither of us yet possessed. So we lived together for a few months and then apart throughout our short marriage. We were in constant communication, and we were always trying to sort it out but struggling with what each of us needed, wanted, or expected. I thought about divorce on occasion, but having been brought up and educated in the Catholic faith, my inherited belief was that marriage was forever. I also believed that if we divorced we would still be married in the eyes of God and that neither of us could ever marry again, unless one of us died. I believed that the choice I had already made was a final one, and I struggled with how I could make it work. I loved him, but I was terribly unhappy with our situation.

The weekend prior to David's accidental death we spent time together trying to sort it out once more. Then two days later he was gone. I felt overwhelming sadness and also guilt that I had even thought of divorce. I blamed myself. I thought that I had made this happen because I didn't want to be married. The depression that followed was a result of all that guilt and shame. I was convinced that I was a bad person for not wanting the traditional relationship I grew up believing I should want. Looking back, I realize that my overwhelming sadness and emotional instability at that time were totally normal due to experiencing the grief of such a deep loss. However, I never questioned my belief system and how that played a part in my feelings of guilt and remorse. It wasn't until my divorce from my second husband many years later, as

I was going through my healing process and reflecting on past unhealed wounds, that I understood that perhaps it was time to release some of those inherited beliefs that were still holding me hostage.

Another of the beliefs I struggled with was the belief that divorce is failure. Divorce statistics always imply "failed" marriages. I don't hear divorce statistics cited as much anymore, or perhaps I choose not to listen, but we've all heard them enough to make many of us feel like failures when we even contemplate divorce. My personal feeling is that relationships and marriage should always be about growth with each partner supporting the other's individual growth, while the relationship deepens in mutual admiration and respect. This is now one of my core beliefs, a belief based on my own experience with marriage and my own transformational healing process.

In addition to believing that relationships are, or should be, about growth, I've also come to see that a breakup often happens in a partnership when one of the partners suddenly begins struggling with a new conflict in their thought process about their life. When one partner begins questioning their own happiness or begins feeling that something is off balance in their relationship, whether justified or not, it plants a seed of change. That seed can then begin to create intense analysis about the relationship. If the relationship can't support it and grow through it, then that intense analysis can lead to a breakup or divorce. Divorce and breakups usually feel like a failure, especially for the partner who has tried so desperately to make it work or has grown up with the belief that marriage is forever. Yet as we know it takes two to make any relationship solid, and one person trying is never enough. Therefore, one of my own personally held beliefs is that a breakup or a divorce is not a failure, any more than the death of a loved one is.

As painful as they are, these life changes are tremendous opportunities for growth. However, we will only grow through these experiences if we consciously allow ourselves to. There are marriages and relationships on each end of the spectrum of course: the good or growing ones on one end, and the toxic ones—filled with addiction, infidelity, and more—on the other end. Then there's the very large segment of relationships in between, the ones of convenience or indifference. Many people stay together for any number of reasons, even when there is no love, and that is a choice each person makes, which is often grounded in their inherited belief system.

What about you? Do you have a belief that's keeping you stuck? It may not be a belief that you are ready or willing to release, now or ever, and that's fine, because it's your choice. It may just be helpful to look at your beliefs and reflect on how they may be affecting your life. You can make the decision to release their hold on you, if you choose to. Any awareness at this point can be freeing. Looking at your life and circumstances from a new perspective can help you see that there are many paths to happiness. It may be time to evaluate what you truly want in your life going forward and whether or not the beliefs you've been holding on to are still assisting you on that path. Are they your true beliefs or simply beliefs you've inherited? Are you living your life in a way that feels good to you, or are you living your life in a way that is expected of you?

Our Beliefs Create Our Behaviors

Our behaviors are also linked to those same neural pathways in our brain, because we are accustomed to reacting in the same way, every time, to the same stimulus, as I explained previously. These responses often are a result of beliefs we have about ourselves and who we are. Many of us have been told over and over again by parents, educators, or even friends certain things about ourselves that we then begin to accept as truth. Perhaps we've been told that we are too sensitive, too open, or too trusting, or perhaps the opposite, that we are not sensitive enough, not open enough, or not trusting enough. Keep in mind that this is someone else's opinion of us and it may not be an accurate depiction of who we really are. However, we have heard it so often that we become accustomed to responding in a certain way.

So consciously changing our beliefs about ourselves or creating new ones is only part of the equation. We still have to be mindful to respond more thoughtfully from our new perspective. In essence, as we grow in awareness and become more thoughtful, compassionate people we may still find ourselves often reacting to situations in a way that has become a "programmed" response rather than a carefully thought out response.

I find this happens in the simplest situations. Imagine as a child being told that your room is always messy; you hear this from your parents and perhaps even your friends. Whether you realize it or not, you often internalize something you are told over and over again about yourself and assume it is fact. It becomes one of your beliefs, so much so that after a while you find that you never do clean your room. Let's face it, you're a kid with so many better things to do and it's really not a big deal to you, so it just becomes part of who you believe you are. You accept it as fact. Now let's say that you have moved out of your parents' home and you're moving into your first apartment, which you furnish and decorate yourself. You're so excited that you want it to look beautiful all the time. You've changed the habit; you're now an organized person, not a messy one. However, that long-held belief can sneak back in if you aren't careful. In no time flat, once the newness wears off, you can easily revert back to who you believe you are based on what you've been told and what you have believed about yourself for so long.

This also happens if we have been overweight for most of our lives, and then we lose weight. The weight loss is more difficult to maintain because of the long-held belief about who we are. We find that we still hold on to the belief that we are an overweight person, and even as we lose weight and get in better shape, we often don't internalize those results into the fabric of who we are now, so we still continue to see ourselves from an old reality. This is why old habits are so hard to break and new ones are so challenging to create, but it's not impossible. We can learn to be mindful of the behaviors we would like to create and then build our new belief systems about ourselves based on who we actually want to be.

One of my own habits that I struggled to break was the habit of being late. I was easily sidetracked as a child and had terrible time-management skills. I remember my mom often said that I had only two speeds: slow and stop. I always struggled with being on time. My belief was that I was a person who always ran late, and this belief was backed by very solid evidence. Therefore, every time I was late for work or an appointment, I would always chastise myself by saying to myself, "I'm always late!"

I struggled with this awful habit for many years, trying hard to break it with limited success. Then one day, many years ago, I was at a business seminar and a speaker was on stage talking about how we perpetuate our own bad habits by what we say to ourselves. I heard her loud and clear. The truth is that when we are told, or even tell ourselves, the same thing over and over again, we internalize that message and it becomes part of our identity. The only way to change a habit is to start telling ourselves a new story, an opposite story. So I learned to change my own habit simply by changing the words I used. It wasn't easy, but I was determined. Every time I was late after that I would catch myself before thinking negatively and say these words to myself: "That's not at all like you to be late, Deborah."

It did feel stupid at first, as I knew that it was very much like me, but with consistent and constant effort I was able to break up that old pathway and reprogram my thinking. I even began teaching this technique in my own presentations and workshops, and my audience loved it and certainly related to it. The bottom line is that I am no longer a person who constantly runs late. Do I occasionally run late? Of course, as many of us do, but I am usually on time and often early to appointments now. I'm proud of that because I worked very hard to change not only the behavior but also the belief that I held about myself. I created a new neural pathway from this new pattern of behavior, and I created a new belief about myself with it: I am a person who honors other people by making every effort to be on time for my appointments with them.

So how does all of this relate to healing your heartache? Well, many of the beliefs we have about ourselves have created programmed behaviors that we have carried with us for years and have even brought with us into our relationships. Those beliefs may now be holding us back as we find ourselves behaving in ways that no longer feel comfortable or authentic to who we are.

Here are some examples of beliefs that we may hold about ourselves, along with what may result from those beliefs:

❖ The belief that we don't make good choices or decisions, which results in always second-guessing ourselves or blaming ourselves.

❖ The belief that we aren't good with finances, which results in being afraid to make a wrong move or trusting others more than ourselves with our own money.

❖ The belief that we must always be in control, which can cause anxiety and exhaustion because we feel we can never relax and let go.

❖ The belief that we must make all the decisions in a relationship, which can result in feeling overwhelmed and resentful of our partner.

These are just a few examples of beliefs that may be causing programmed responses and limiting us in our lives.

So what behaviors would you like to change? Would you like to be less reactive and more easygoing, or perhaps less easygoing and more decisive? Whatever it is, I would like to challenge you to think about it now as you work through the following exercise.

An Awareness Exercise

To help you focus on whatever behavior you may want to change, I'm going to ask you to work on five questions. To assist you with this exercise I'll use an example from my own life first. Here is an example of a behavior that I needed to change to help myself move forward.

1. What behavior or habit do I have that I would like to change?

   I want to change the habit that I have to be in control and make all of the major decisions in my relationships.

2. Is that behavior or habit rooted in a belief about myself?

   Yes, my belief is that my marriage would fall apart if I wasn't in control.

3. Where did that belief come from?

   My belief came from the fact that my partner told me that making decisions about money stressed him out. In addition, he had an addictive personality, and I worried that he wouldn't make the best decisions. So I became the main decision maker by default.

4. Why would I like to change or modify that behavior?

   Having to make all the decisions was overwhelming and I felt exhausted by the responsibility.

5. When I do exhibit that behavior, what can I say to myself in a very positive way to begin to tell a new story of who I want to truly be?

I can tell myself that it's okay to relax and not feel that I have to control every decision in a relationship. I can remind myself that a relationship consists of two people making decisions together and that we are partners, so not everything is my responsibility.

Now it's your turn. Take a few minutes to work through these questions for yourself. Give yourself time to reflect on what may be causing you discomfort in your life at this moment and what programmed behaviors you may be able to consciously modify to ease that discomfort. Contemplating these questions can be such a powerful way to begin to examine some of your long-held beliefs and behaviors.

1. What behavior or habit do I have that I would like to change?

_____

_____

_____

2. Is that behavior or habit rooted in a belief about myself?

_____

_____

_____

3. Where did that belief come from?

_____

_____

_____

4. Why would I like to change or modify that behavior?

_____

_____

_____

5. When I do exhibit that behavior, what can I say to myself in a very positive way to begin to tell a new story of who I want to truly be?

_____

_____

_____

You have the opportunity to re-create yourself in the world any time you choose to. Whatever has happened in your life does not have to define you. This is your life, and it's totally up to you how you choose to present yourself going forward. Be brave and be the absolute best you can be. Examining your beliefs and behaviors will help you gain a deeper understanding of yourself. It will also help you heal the emotions that may still feel trapped inside of you right now. This is just the beginning of creating the awareness within you that you really do have the power to work through this transition and heal your heartache.

STEP 3

Accept Your Present

In the first step of this H-E-A-R-T Process I encouraged you to truly honor your feelings. I suggested ways to face both the emotional pain and the physical pain you've been suffering by sharing your pain with a professional or with a friend, or through your writing at the very least. That first step is so important because we can only work through what we are willing to see and acknowledge. It's where you begin to accept that healing needs to take place in order to move forward. Then in the second step of this process I encouraged you to take a look at your long-held beliefs and behaviors, and examine them more closely. This will help you find more awareness and a deeper understanding of what old beliefs about your life or yourself may be keeping you stuck in your pain. Now I want to applaud you for still being here with me and being open to this next step in the process.

The simple fact is that you suddenly find yourself here

in this particular place in your life, and you're in need of some relief. I understand that because I was right where you are. Yes, we all have our particular circumstances, but the pain we feel is so similar because the heartache is real. Unfortunately, we can't change the past; we can only deal with this present moment, so I'm going to suggest ways that will help you begin to accept where you are right now. My goal is to help you feel a bit lighter, because I know how heavy this space can seem when you're sad.

This is not an overnight fix, but it will work if you're willing to step just a little outside of your comfort zone. It may feel hard at first to push yourself, but it won't be difficult if you truly want to feel some relief and a sense of peace in your life again. I'm simply asking you to be willing to help yourself a bit, and in the process, you can reap the rewards of eventually finding your way back to a life filled with peace and even joy.

Acknowledge and Accept

The first step in moving forward from this spot is acknowledging where you are and accepting it. I know that sounds rough. It certainly did to me. I wanted my old life back; I wanted "us" back, who we were together when everything was light and lovely. However, I had no choice but to move forward and create a new reality for myself. I had to find peace of mind; my life and my sanity depended upon it.

Lao Tzu said, *"If you are depressed, you are living in the past. If you are anxious, you are living in the future. If you are at peace, you are living in the present."* Finding peace in the midst of change and transition isn't easy, especially when it either wasn't our choice or we feel we had no choice. However, living in the present moment is the only way to find peace. We know that it's so much easier to let our minds wander to the past and fall back into sadness about what we've lost. It's also easy to allow our thoughts about the future to create more worry and anxiety. Therefore, staying in the present moment will require some real focus. Peace comes from within. It's up to us to surround ourselves with positive, supportive people and to find ways to nurture our souls.

Take a moment to reflect on these questions and then journal your answers:

1. Who are the people in your life that you feel most supported by?

   _____

   _____

   _____

2. What can you do to spend more time with these people?

_____

_____

_____

3. Who are the people in your life that you feel least supported by?

_____

_____

_____

4. How can you manage to spend less time with them?

_____

_____

_____

5. What are some of the things that nurture your soul?

_____

_____

_____

6. What keeps you very present in the moment?

_____

_____

_____

7. What makes you feel at peace?

_____

_____

_____

8. What have you always wanted to try?

_____

_____

_____

9. What have you often thought about learning?

_____

_____

_____

10. What is one step that you can take today to nurture your soul?

_____

_____

_____

Meditation

One of the practices that nurtures my soul, keeps me present in the moment, and brings me peace is meditation. When I pray, I know that I'm speaking directly to God or Spirit; however, when I meditate I feel that I'm simply being with God or Spirit. Both are extremely powerful, and both are a path to inner peace. Many of us have grown up learning to pray, but very few of us ever learned to meditate as children. That's beginning to change, as some educational systems are actually teaching meditation to young students in the classroom as a tool they can use to calm themselves when they feel stressed.

At first most of my clients are convinced that it will be a struggle for them to quiet their mind and silence their thoughts. However, in meditation the goal is not to silence our thoughts, but to simply allow them to arise and then dissolve, or float by, on their own. Meditation is not an escape from reality, but rather a way of seeing reality with more clarity and a deeper understanding. That's why it's so powerful when we include meditation in our healing process; it allows us to develop that sense of inner freedom that only comes with being fully present in this moment.

If you have never meditated my suggestion is to go to YouTube and search for meditation videos, and start with guided meditations, where a narrator is taking you on a peaceful journey. You can also begin the way I did by just sitting quietly and counting your breaths. Remember the goal is not to try to silence your thoughts, but rather to not focus on them when they appear and let them simply drift by.

Spending time in nature is also an incredible way to clear the negative thoughts from your head, get in touch with your higher self, and feel whole again. The point is that there are so many ways to de-stress and move our thoughts away from the negative chatter that constantly goes on in our heads when we're sad, angry, fearful, or feeling forced into a change we didn't want.

Here are a number of suggestions that can help you begin to calm that negative chatter and make it easier to live in present moment awareness:

❖ Pray or meditate.

❖ Walk on the beach or hike in nature and soak in all of the beauty.

❖ Gaze at a starlit sky and imagine the vastness of the universe.

❖ Read an inspirational book.

❖ Play with your pets and be present for them.

❖ Look into the eyes of a child and give them your full attention.

❖ Listen to uplifting music and dance with abandon.

❖ Watch films that can't help but make you laugh.

❖ Work out with weights and feel your muscles get stronger and leaner.

❖ Practice yoga and feel yourself develop more balance and inner strength.

❖ Learn a language you've always wanted to learn.

❖ Start a gratitude journal and list at least seven things each morning you are grateful for.

❖ Take voice lessons or begin learning a musical instrument.

❖ Join a tennis, pickleball, or racquetball club, and play at least once a week.

❖ Take a class in something creative like art, sculpture, or dance just for the fun of it.

❖ Make a new friend at the gym, on your walks, or in one of your classes and go for coffee.

❖ Join a new club or meet-up group and find a new tribe of friends to associate with.

❖ Volunteer at an animal rescue, a soup kitchen, a senior center, a children's hospital, or a veterans organization.

❖ Make someone smile . . . it may be the highlight of their day.

Now reread this list and notice which ideas catch your attention. That's your starting point. Even if it's only one idea, do it now, or make the commitment to yourself to start tomorrow. Take the first step. Nothing can change if you aren't willing to try, so be brave and flex that courage muscle again. It gets stronger every time, and it gets easier as well. It's up to you to create an environment for your healing. Who you become on the other side of this transition is totally up to you and you alone. Don't be afraid of that. You're so much stronger than you know. You simply feel worn down because of all that's happened.

Our bodies take a beating when we go through major life transitions, but we are also incredibly resilient, if we only allow ourselves to be. There is nothing more empowering than rising up from the ashes to become the glorious person you were meant to be and have been all along! That part of your journey begins right now. Accept where you are at this very moment and make it the best moment you can, by taking baby steps each day. Before you know it, you'll feel lighter.

This is only the beginning. When we allow ourselves to discover the strength that is within us, it spreads throughout our body and outside of us as well. It encompasses our entire aura. We respond to every situation differently, and other people respond to us differently as well. Finding our own sense of strength and inner peace is transforming, and it has the ability to transform our lives.

STEP 4

Release Your Past

This is perhaps the hardest step of all, but it will be the most rewarding when you finally get to the other side of it. This is where you get to sift out what is no longer serving you in your life. It's difficult because most of us hate to let go of anything. Think about how many things you probably have in your closet that you never wear or in your kitchen or garage that you never use. Most of us find that letting go of a favorite old shirt or a pair of jeans that are worn, too tight, or out of style is difficult enough. Now I'm going to ask you to begin to let go of those worn-out beliefs that you are still clinging so tightly to.

Remember the beliefs we examined in the second step of this H-E-A-R-T Process? It's time now to decide if you want to continue to hold on to them and stay in sadness, anger, or fear, or if perhaps it's time to release them so you can find your own true north. I'm asking you to be courageous. I'm asking you this because I know that courage is the main ingredient you need to move forward. To create the life you want, you have to decide to become the very best version of yourself. Most people never take that step. They live their life moving from day to day, allowing circumstances and other people's agendas to determine who they are. That's their decision. That's their choice. It's no longer your choice though, not if you sincerely want to move forward.

I remind myself often that where I am right now is exactly where I'm supposed to be. It's really the only place I can be given all of the choices I've made in my life up to this point. I remember doing a presentation and saying to the audience, "Wherever you are right now is exactly where you are supposed to be." A man at the seminar later approached me saying that he had heard that said before and he didn't understand it at all. His wife had left him for another man, and he was in deep emotional pain. He couldn't possibly see how he was "supposed to be" in this place. He hired me as his coach, and throughout our working together he has come to a deeper understanding of that phrase. He can now see how his marriage ending has actually served his higher good. He feels more relaxed in his life now than he did when he was married. He's finding more contentment within himself, and he seems more peaceful.

When we're in the midst of things, we can't always see clearly. Even if the situation is bad or uncomfortable, we find it familiar so we often stay. It isn't until we're outside of a situation that we can truly analyze it and see it with more clarity.

When change happens, we often find ourselves asking WHY questions:

❖ "Why did this happen to me?"

❖ "Why am I alone?"

❖ "Why did this have to happen now?"

❖ "Why didn't I see this coming?"

❖ "Why didn't I prepare for this?"

We also tend to ask ourselves WHAT questions:

❖ "What did I do wrong?"

❖ "What did I not see?"

❖ "What should I have done differently?"

❖ "What did I not understand?"

❖ "What's wrong with me?"

The truth is that I have asked myself these same questions too many times. I've also asked myself, "What if I had opened my eyes sooner? Dealt with this sooner? Become the person I wanted to be sooner? Followed my dreams sooner? Written my book sooner?" The reality, however, is that I am where I am, and it's exactly where I am supposed to be at this moment. I opened my eyes and saw what was happening in my life at exactly the right moment, when I was ready and willing to deal with it. I couldn't write this book or become this person until I got to this exact place in my life with these experiences behind me. It's all divine timing, and although it may feel far from perfect right now, it actually is the right time for you as well.

How do I know that it's the right time for you? Because you're still here with me reading these words and trying to find some comfort. We can take the worst things that have ever happened in our lives and turn them into our biggest opportunities for growth and self-discovery.

Forgiving Others

When I suggest that it's time to release your past, what am I asking you to release exactly? In addition to those beliefs and behaviors that may still be holding you back,

I'm also encouraging you to release the people you are holding hostage in your heart. The people we have loved deeply are still within our hearts, even when they have died, walked away, or driven us away by their actions. They are still in our hearts and we have to release them in order to heal. In doing so we also release the hold those painful memories have over us. That doesn't mean we lose the beautiful memories; it just means that right now we need to find a way to forgive. There it is, that word most of us don't want to think about, let alone deal with. However, we have to deal with it because not doing so holds us hostage as well. Forgiveness is freedom.

When my first husband died, I didn't understand much of this, but intuitively I knew that I had to forgive him for leaving me all alone to figure everything out. David was the first man I'd ever loved, and he was also my best friend. Although we were very confused about how to proceed in our marriage, he knew me better than anyone ever had. Then he was gone. I was angry at him for deserting me, and I was angry at myself. Forgiving him was the easiest part and forgiving myself was the hardest. Years later when Ken and I were going through our divorce, all of those feelings resurfaced. I realized then that there were other people I needed to forgive as well. I needed to forgive all of the people who were in my life when my first husband died who didn't realize how depressed I was, so they didn't know how to be there for me, and I didn't know how to ask them to.

However, years later as I went through the divorce I learned how to ask for help. Yet even then I only confided in the friends I knew would understand what I was feeling, wouldn't judge me, and I could feel safe with. As I forgave myself and Ken, I also forgave all the people who didn't know what to say or thought that what they were saying was helping when so often it wasn't. None of us are perfect. We can be there for friends who later may not be able to or even know how to be there for us, and it is forgivable. Forgiving helps us more than it ever helps the one we forgive, because it releases us from the prison of anger and hurt that surrounds our hearts.

We've all felt judged. When we are going through a life transition, it can seem like everyone in the world has an opinion of how we should behave or what our next move should be. When Ken and I were going through our divorce, we were trying to maintain a friendship, which was extremely difficult under the circumstances. It worked for a while, and then I needed to pull away for a time and later we were able to build that friendship again. However, that was our process and certainly not the norm.

One evening at a friend's home, during the early stage

of our divorce process, we gave each other a hug and almost immediately my friend said to us, "You certainly don't act like a couple who are getting divorced!" It felt sarcastic and judgmental to us, but we tried to laugh it off. We discussed it later and decided to release the judgment we felt coming from my friend, as we knew that there was no way she could possibly understand our relationship. All relationships are unique, because they are a combination of two unique individuals. So how can any of us understand the inner workings of another couple's partnership? This certainly wasn't the last time someone would express an opinion of how we should act or be at the end of our marriage, or even beyond, but it didn't matter. All that mattered to us was how we felt and how we wanted this relationship to end or transform.

I love the phrase "Whatever someone else thinks of me is none of my business." I repeat that phrase to myself often. The truth is that what people think of us really has nothing to do with us. It has everything to do with them, with their own fears, their own beliefs, and their own insecurities. It serves us well to remember that, and it helps us to stay true to who we are. Remember you are unique, not a copy or a blueprint of what someone else expects you to be. You are a miracle, and the world needs you to be exactly who you are.

Forgiving Ourselves

It's hard to forgive another when we haven't yet forgiven ourselves. We have to be willing to accept the fact that we're not perfect, that we did the best we could under the circumstances, and that we're doing the best we can right now as well. We can only hold ourselves responsible to a point. Just as we often say about our parents, "They did the best they could with the knowledge and resources they had," so did we as partners. We can't love fully until we are able to love ourselves fully. Why is that? Because if we don't love ourselves then we believe ourselves to be unlovable, and why would we ever believe that someone else could truly love us? So it works the same with forgiveness. We can't forgive in another what we aren't willing to forgive in ourselves.

If we're totally honest we can see that, deep down, we may be angry at ourselves. We may blame ourselves in some way for what happened, even if that seems ridiculous at times and even if we feel that we did nothing wrong. It's vital in this step to really dig down into your feelings about yourself and see what comes up. I'm going to ask you a series of questions to get you started. Journaling your answers can really help you here. Yes, I know that your partner may have left you feeling abandoned or betrayed, or they may have died, but right now this is about you and what you are feeling about yourself.

So take a moment to reflect on these questions. Writing down what comes up as you do can be very enlightening and cathartic. Keep in mind that not all of these questions may relate to your particular situation, so simply ignore any that don't apply.

1. Do you feel in any way responsible for what happened?

_____

_____

_____

2. If so, why do you feel this way?

_____

_____

_____

3. Did you see something you chose to ignore or hoped would work out on its own?

_____

_____

_____

4. If so, what was it and why do you think you chose to respond that way?

_____

_____

_____

5. Did you ignore signs that may have hinted of things to come?

_____

_____

_____

6. If yes, why do you feel you chose to ignore those signs?

_____

_____

_____

7. Did you set healthy boundaries in your relationship, and did you stick to them?

_____

_____

_____

8. If not, why not?

_____

_____

_____

9. Were you communicative enough with your partner about what you needed and expected in your relationship?

_____

_____

_____

10. If not, why not?

_____

_____

_____

11. Were you willing to compromise or do you feel that you compromised too much?

_____

_____

_____

12. What emotion does that bring up for you right now, and why?

_____

_____

_____

13. Were you true to yourself in this relationship?

_____

_____

_____

14. If not, why do you think that was?

_____

_____

_____

15. If you could choose to do anything differently going forward, what would that be and why?

_____

_____

_____

These are tough questions, so go back over them again and really allow yourself the time for reflection. I realize this isn't an easy process, but healing your heartache is worth it. So dig in, and you'll gain a deeper understanding of yourself. Forgiveness has to start with us forgiving ourselves first, if only because we may have assumed that we could control everything in our lives. Unfortunately, the only thing we can really control is our own attitude, and that begins with examining our thoughts.

Once you work through your feelings about yourself, it will be easier to accept the fact that you're actually perfect in your imperfections. What I mean by this is you are a child of God or Spirit or Universal Wisdom, and so you are a perfect being. However, the fact that you're here in human form with free will means that you will have choices to make and challenges to overcome. Because of our humanity, we are not always going to make the right choices and we are not always going to behave perfectly. So it means that we need to learn to forgive ourselves, and in doing so we learn to forgive others in their humanness as well.

When we learn how to forgive others, our lives become so much easier. We realize then that the offhand comment someone made or the air of judgment we felt is more of a reflection of that person's feelings and beliefs about themselves and their own life than it is about us. Forgiveness will flow more easily as we see that. We can make the choice to not associate with certain people we don't feel good around, and sometimes that's our best option. However, for the people we desire to keep in our lives we can learn to speak our truth with compassion and allow them the opportunity to grow along with us. This is where we become truly empowered, when we can sift through our experiences and release the negative ones and the negative people as well. Our lives begin to feel lighter, and although we might not yet feel joyful, we begin to sense that joy is out there, just waiting for us to allow it back in.

STEP 5

Transform Your Thoughts
to Transform Your Life

This is my favorite step in the H-E-A-R-T Process, because this is where we get to see how powerful we truly are. We have the ability to change our attitude about everything in our lives, by learning to adjust our thoughts. Once we begin to align our thoughts with the direction we'd like our lives to take, our lives begin to change as if by magic. The truth is we often make changes in our lives so much more difficult than they have to be because we continue to believe and respond as we always have. We've already discussed this, and I hope you're beginning to see how releasing old beliefs and behaviors, while creating new habits of thoughts and responses, is a major key to moving forward and creating your best life possible.

I do know how difficult it is to get out of that sad place when we've been there for so long. It may not be a comfortable place, but it does become more familiar the longer we're there. So I'm asking you to listen to this with an open mind because I'm trying to offer you some relief. Because our bodies are made up of pure energy, how we feel in any given moment is creating a particular energy within us. That particular energy, also referred to as a vibration, tends to attract similar energy. Therefore, when we feel sad, all of our thoughts are going to be sad ones, and the more we think those thoughts, the more sad thoughts we will continue to think. It sounds terribly simple, and it is. The way it works is that once we're in the mode or attitude of sadness or fear, our minds begin to continue that process, and now we begin thinking more thoughts that match the original thought. We then begin to feel even worse. However, it works with happy thoughts as well . . . and that's really exciting!

Learning to Pivot

I'm going to encourage you to use a technique called pivoting. Politicians are experts at this when they're being interviewed by the media. When they're asked a question they don't want to answer, they immediately pivot to a different subject. It's actually fascinating to watch how adept they are at this technique. They have to be I suppose, as they're always being bombarded by media questions that they may not be prepared for, and they have to be able to think on their feet very quickly. However, this skill can also be very helpful to us. Learning to pivot, when we're feeling bad, can be the key to changing our vibration. It can be an emotional lifesaver.

Let me give you an example. When I was going through my divorce, I was terribly sad. I kept remembering how beautiful our relationship had been for so long. I found myself thinking about "us" and all the wonderful times when we were so happy together. The loss of that relationship was devastating to me, so whenever I reflected on those beautiful memories I couldn't help but feel sadder and sadder. It was as if I was in a downward spiral with one beautiful memory reminding me of another, and then of the horrific loss I was feeling. My vibration was so low that I couldn't stop crying. The waves of sadness would overtake me, and I felt totally out of control.

It was then that I reached for a number of fabulous books; one of them was *Ask and It Is Given* by Esther and Jerry Hicks. In this book they discuss a scale of emotions. They list twenty-two different types of emotions on this scale with fear, grief, depression, despair, and powerlessness on the bottom and working upward through emotions like anger, blame, doubt, disappointment, hopefulness, and optimism, all the way up to joy, knowledge, empowerment, freedom, love, and appreciation at the top of the scale. The idea is that the higher the vibration of the emotion, the better we feel.

It became clear to me that when I felt grief and depression my vibration was just about as low as it could get. However, if I could "pivot" to another thought, even one that made me feel anger or blame, my vibration would be higher, and I would actually begin to feel some relief. I now explain this to my clients this way. I have come to see sadness, fear, depression, and despair as very passive emotions. It's hard to be in forward motion while feeling these emotions; however, anger and blame are more active. So we are actually feeling more empowered in anger than we are in sadness or fear.

Let me illustrate this with the following example: Imagine that we are walking down the street in the evening and hear a sound behind us. If we become fearful that someone may be following us to cause us harm, then we tend to freeze in that emotion of fear. However, if we become angry that someone may be trying to intimidate or harm us, then our emotions are more heightened and we begin to take more of an active stance, preparing ourselves and becoming more vigilant than we would be if we were frozen by fear.

That's what I'm saying when I suggest that you learn to pivot. So, when you catch yourself feeling sadness and despair, take a moment to stop and reflect on the thoughts you are thinking that are causing that emotion. Then turn your thoughts to something different. For example, when I felt overwhelming sadness I would try very hard to pivot and begin thinking about how my beautiful marriage falling apart made me angry, at him for his drinking, or at myself for enabling him. It almost didn't matter where I directed my anger at that point. It was just important to pivot away from the passive emotion of sadness and despair to the active emotion of anger or blame. In this way I felt more empowered realizing that I did in fact have control over my thoughts and my attitude. That gave me hope that I could actually find my way to the other side of this heartache.

I remember explaining this process in a workshop, and a woman remarked that her therapist had told her that she should try to work through her anger, rather than hold on to it. I told her I absolutely agree with that, but that first we have to get to the point where we can face our anger in order to deal with it and heal it. So I'm not suggesting that anger is a good place to be for very long; however, I am suggesting that it's a good place to rise to from our sadness, depression, and fear. I have seen too many people stay in those lower vibrations for far too long, and that's when we begin to feel hopeless. I want to help you rise out of that dark place and feel empowered to take back your life!

Telling Yourself a New Story

What are you currently attracting in your life? What we attract is a mirror of our own thoughts and feelings about ourselves. When we feel worthy and valued we attract the people and situations that match that. If you work on loving and valuing yourself first, then you'll find that the people walking into your life will mirror that as well.

Remember, the words we say are powerful and an outward reflection of how we're feeling. When we're unhappy or we feel hopeless we tend to speak in negative words and phrases, reflecting our hopelessness and frustration with our lives. However, when we're feeling unhappy, but we're actively trying to stay hopeful, our words express more positivity, and that leads to more positive experiences in our lives.

Telling ourselves a new story is a very powerful way to manifest a better life. When we've been through a personal trauma of any kind it's natural to repeat our story to our family and friends. Many of us even process our emotions that way. It's also natural to repeat our story to ourselves, in our own thoughts, often over and over again. This may be helpful for a time, as it enables us to face and honor our feelings. However, it can be dangerous to stay stuck in that sad or angry story for an extended period. The fact is that our body is also processing our emotions as we feel them. The emotions of sadness, anger and fear can cause a tremendous amount of stress. Each time we relive the experience of trauma, by speaking about it or dwelling on it, we're creating additional stress in our body, and stress can be a catalyst for disease.

A clear example of this happened in my own life. Three years after my divorce I was beginning to feel more like myself again. I was feeling lighter and enjoying my life more. I'd worked through so much of my emotional healing process, made new friends and I was welcoming new experiences. Then one evening, as I was driving home from having dinner with friends, I began feeling uncomfortably odd. I felt strangely nauseous, with a slight ache in the middle of my forehead. I remember reflecting on what I had eaten that evening: grilled salmon, broccoli, and a glass of red wine. I wondered if something I'd ingested was causing this discomfort. A few minutes later I felt a horrible sensation of pain in my right breast as if I'd been kicked by a mule. Within minutes the pain hit the middle of my chest and I reached for my cell phone. I heard myself say to the 911 operator, "I think I'm having a heart attack." I pulled off the road to wait for the ambulance, as the pain suddenly radiated into my back as well.

My story has a happy ending. I'm one of the lucky ones and I'm now blessed with incredible health. However, the fact is I was always in good physical condition, even prior to this incident. I was working as a Health Coach at the time, eating extremely well, in great shape and on no medications. The cardiologist at the hospital initially didn't believe that I could have had a heart attack, especially after looking at me, my blood work and my clean medical history. He was totally confused by my case and told me that nothing about it made sense to him. My friends and clients, who knew me so well, were also shocked. However, I now know what triggered this episode: for many months, after my divorce, I would tell my friends and myself, over and over again, that my heart was broken. Even though I was no longer speaking those words, I had told that same sad story for far too long.

We all have predispositions to disease, whether through genetics or through carcinogens we've ingested. My father had heart disease; I inhaled second-hand smoke while singing in jazz clubs for years; I have mercury fillings. However, stress is a major contributor to disease. I'd suffered through depression at the end of each of my marriages, and tried to handle it on my own each time. This time it caught up with me. Repeating the words "my heart is broken" certainly didn't help.

I now tell a different story. I talk about the lessons I've learned from my life experiences. I repeat the words "I love my life" very often, and when people ask how I am, my response is usually, "I'm fabulous, thank you!" I know how powerful my words are. I have truly learned that lesson.

So how can you begin to tell yourself a new story? First of all, you must be very aware of the words you're speaking and the thoughts you're thinking. Each time you relate your story, you must find a way to somehow create a positive ending. In other words, how can you make your story into a catalyst for a new and better life? As you tell your story, can you also relate what you've learned about yourself? Can you share how your life is moving forward because of your new awareness? Anything you can do to tell a new and more positive story will help you heal. It will also help you attract all of the things you truly deserve into your life.

Living in Gratitude

I know that you have heard this before, and I even suggested starting a gratitude journal in the third step. However, I'm saying something different here. If you want to transform your life, you have to transform your thinking first. There is no other way. The thoughts you think will always create your reality, every time, whether you believe it or not. So I'm now suggesting that you work on living in gratitude each and every day. I'm suggesting that you become so present to the moment that you notice the sky and the stars. I'm encouraging you to look into the eyes of a child or a pet as they look at you and feel their innocence. I'm asking you to really see the people you encounter every day and pay attention. So often we go through the line at the supermarket or pharmacy, and although we may say thank you as we walk away, we often don't take the time to really look closely at those people.

So how do you begin? When you go out today or tomorrow, I'm asking you to notice your environment, the weather, the roads, the scenery, and the people, with a more heightened sense of awareness. Just pay more attention and really "see" the people you meet. Look into their eyes when they speak to you, and think about how wonderful it is to be able to interact with them. There are people who can never leave their homes or drive a car or walk into a store or see the view, the sun, or the clouds. We have the opportunity to do so much, and we take most of it for granted. So "living in gratitude" is more than listing the things we're grateful for. It's about being grateful for everything. It's about totally living in this moment and really appreciating all that it is.

"Living in gratitude" means allowing life to bring us the lessons that enable us to grow and become more. It means accepting that everything that has happened in our lives is somehow a blessing, even if it seems to be disguised as pain in this moment. It means that we truly release our assumptions of what life should be and instead we allow it to unfold naturally. "Living in gratitude" opens our eyes wider and increases our awareness of all that life is and can be. It frees us from the bondage of trying to control every outcome and enables us to make better choices based on our heightened awareness and intuition. We are able to appreciate more, to be more open to love, and to live more fully present in this moment.

I recently watched a movie about a small group of people who had survived a plane crash in which everyone else had perished. They were dealing with so many fearful and confusing emotions, and there was a therapist who had been asked to help them. They were each struggling with the pain of the accident in a different way. However, at the end of the movie, it turned out that none of them had actually survived. They had in fact all perished and were spirits trying to understand what had happened to them. Even the therapist had been a casualty on the flight, but she didn't remember that she was even on the flight. It was such an emotional ending that I immediately felt a sense of gratitude that I was still living my life and still had time to accomplish things, to enjoy my friends and family, to laugh, and to love. That's what "living in gratitude" is all about, and you have the ability to create that in your life every single day. So why not start now?

Don't waste a precious moment of this beautiful life. Be willing to do the work that it takes to heal your heartache. You have so much more love to give the world and so much more joy to experience. Don't waste any more time on the past. Embrace the beautiful memories you've had and know that each day you live you have the opportunity to create even more of them. The one thing that is inevitable is change. If you allow that change to be the catalyst for your growth and transformation, your future can be brighter than you've ever imagined.

3

Living in
New Awareness

"Pay attention to the cracks,
because that's where the light gets in."

—Leonard Cohen

As I said in the introduction, I don't have all the answers, certainly not for your life and not even for mine. We're all a work in progress for as long as we're here. We owe it to ourselves to keep asking ourselves the tough questions to get the answers that will help us move forward and create the life we not only desire but deserve. Did you get that? You *deserve* a fabulous life, but you alone can claim it. As a coach, my job is to help my clients claim their fabulous life. I ask the tough questions to help them go deep into their own thoughts, and I hold the space for them to feel safe.

I won't tell you that I know exactly how you feel because I don't, as our experiences are all as individual as we are. However, I've walked a similar path, and I've done the healing. The steps I've laid out for you are the steps I took in my process. Working through this process enabled me to find my way out of my own pain. It was only then, after careful reflection, that I was able to put those steps together in a logical order. Even as I was going through my own healing, I knew that I would eventually want to help others through theirs as well because it was such a heart-wrenching experience for me. My desire in writing this book was very simply to help you feel better and give you hope that you can heal your heartache and open yourself up to all that your life can become.

It is no accident that the steps of my H-E-A-R-T Process are based on the word "HEART" as I wanted to create something that was easy for you to remember.

❖ **H**onor Your Feelings

❖ **E**xamine Your Beliefs

❖ **A**ccept Your Present

❖ **R**elease Your Past

❖ **T**ransform Your Thoughts to Transform Your Life

My sincere wish is that you've begun to feel more hopeful. There is so much inspiration all around us. We can walk through our lives as if we are sleepwalking, or we can open our eyes wide and see the beauty of it all. There can even be beauty in times of sadness. When I knew I was losing my dad, I felt tremendous sadness. Yet at the same time, I had an overwhelming sense of peace because in my heart I knew that he had lived a long and wonderful life. He was clearly tired and ready to leave. I admit that it isn't as easy to feel that way when we've lost someone too soon or when we've lost a life partner. What we can do, however, is reflect on their life and on our lives with them and focus on the joy and love we shared and allow that to bring us peace. The most important thing is not what has happened in our lives, but rather how we respond to what has happened in our lives.

I used to try to manage or handle my sadness, worry, or stress. I no longer do that. I've come to realize that trying to manage or handle those emotions is just another way of trying to control them and that can cause havoc in our bodies and in our lives. We think we have control, but those emotions are still causing negativity and fear within us. Finding a way to release or even reduce the sadness, worry, and stress is what truly sets us free, and thus allows the solutions to our toughest challenges to appear.

So how will you know when you've begun to heal your heartache? Contemplating these questions and journaling the answers may help you reflect on how well you're doing with your healing process. The last two questions refer more to a breakup or divorce, so ignore those that don't apply to your situation:

1. Are you feeling content with yourself?

_____

_____

_____

2. Do you feel a sense of peace when you're alone?

_____

_____

_____

3. Do you feel gratefulness about your life and in awe of the beauty surrounding you?

_____

_____

_____

4. Have you released your sadness, anger, or fear surrounding the past relationship?

_____

_____

_____

5. Are you able to reflect on the happy memories without getting sad or depressed?

_____

_____

_____

6. Have you found reasons to appreciate that relationship in spite of any negative aspects?

_____

_____

_____

7. Have you learned the lessons from that relationship, so that it won't be necessary to repeat them?

_____

_____

_____

Answering yes to these questions is a good indicator that you are healing your heartache. Answering no to any of them may mean that you need to investigate that aspect a bit deeper to create true healing. The good news is that the H-E-A-R-T Process will help you to do just that, as long as you are willing to take the time to work through it.

You have an opportunity to create the life you want right here and right now. I've tried to give you a roadmap to follow. The important part is to keep moving forward. Just keep trying by taking whatever steps you need to.

Decide what you want your life to look like and feel like. There are no limits, except the ones we impose upon ourselves. I imagine my life as a grand adventure and as a story that I get to write each and every day. I have always felt that way, except when I was sad from the loss of a loved one in my life. That's when I had to be gentle with myself and allow myself the time to grieve, regroup, and heal. That's what I'm trying to help you to do as well.

It's time to be gentle with yourself. So just begin, at the beginning again if you need to. There is no time limit, but there is an incredible life waiting for you on the other side of this heartache. You may have a hard time believing that at this moment, but why not dispel that disbelief for a bit and just try this process anyway.

This book is meant as an outline to start you off. You can work through each of these steps again, taking more time, even days or weeks, on each step. Take as long as you need. The more you work on this process, the more you'll begin to create those new patterns of beliefs and positive behaviors that will serve you for the rest of your life.

Remember to ask for help if you need it, and feel free to reach out to me as well. We all need support from time to time. We may be magnificent, but we're still only human. This being human is an incredible gift though. We get to create our lives one day and one step at a time.

Please don't lose sight of that. You are a powerful creator and this is your life. So just begin, again and again if you must.

Your own healing can be a gift to the world. When you allow yourself to heal and grow and shine, you become an inspiration. Your example will inspire others to believe that they can heal as well. By giving yourself the gift of healing, you also pass it on, and that in itself is such a blessing to all of those around you. It's called the ripple effect. It's like a stone thrown into the middle of a pond. The ripples caused by that one small stone can be seen spreading wider and wider. You can have that effect on others as well. By healing your heartache and allowing joy back into your life you will become such a blessing to everyone you encounter. My wish for you is that you see how powerful you truly are and that you claim that power, beginning right now, to create the fabulous life you deserve.

Acknowledgments

It was my mom who first surrounded me with fabulous books, causing me to fall in love with the written word. I love her deeply, and I thank her for encouraging my writing as well as my independent spirit. I'm also grateful to my dad and I miss him every single day. He was the most honest and authentic man I've ever met. His example has inspired me to release self-judgement and to allow who I am to come through in my writing, and in my life.

I thank my stepdaughter, Marisa Burkhart, my sister Sheri Paiva, and my niece, Alisha Paiva, for their constant love, and a very special thank-you to Alisha for designing this beautiful book cover. To Carol Killman Rosenberg and Gary Rosenberg, "The Book Couple," I offer my sincere gratitude for guiding me throughout this project with incredible skill and patience. I'm also sincerely grateful to Lesley Stone for her meticulous proofreading skills.

I thank all of my dear friends for their friendship, encouragement, and belief in me. In addition, I extend a very special thank-you to my friend Lee Perkins for his incredible support throughout this process and throughout my life. The endless hours of conversation we've had have meant more than I can ever say.

Lastly, I would not have had the courage to pour my heart into these pages without the constant encouragement of Ken Burkhart. He has been my biggest cheerleader from the moment we met, and I've been his. We've been partners and collaborators in music for many years, and I feel grateful to have journeyed through so much of my life with him. We've also endured many tough lessons together, but the faith and unconditional love that is eternally between us have always eased the pain and allowed the joy to eventually shine through again. This has been a true gift in my life.

About the Author

Deborah Paiva is a Board Certified Life Coach, Speaker, Author, and Jazz Vocalist with an incredible passion for life. She inherited her love of books from her mother, and in her twenties, she began focusing on self-discovery and any writing that made her question her existence or purpose. She was drawn to life coaching after going through her own multiple transformations: the death of her first husband when she was only twenty-one years old, major career changes and location moves, and then her divorce from her second husband after many happy years together. One of her greatest joys now is to support others through their own transformations.

As a life coach, Deborah partners with her clients to assist them through various transitions, including divorce, breakup, loss of a loved one, stress reduction, career changes and life balance, as well as helping them expand their creativity and passion in their life. She works with her clients to assist them in discovering their own motivations and helps them work through their obstacles, so they can create the life they envision. She has partnered with hundreds of clients of both genders over the past several years, both privately and in conjunction with numerous medical practices in South Florida. She is committed to helping people create healthier, happier lives for themselves.

As a speaker, Deborah is dynamic and passionate. Her presentations are filled with positive, practical information that her audience is able to immediately use to enhance their lives and well-being. She does presentations and workshops for numerous venues including corporate events, women's expos, singles' events, spiritual expos, networking events and retreats.

She currently lives a joyful and passionate life in South Florida.

Email Deborah at DeborahPaiva111@gmail.com

For more information on Deborah, her services, upcoming events and online workshops, please visit her website: **www.DeborahPaiva.com**

A Gift for You

To thank you for reading this book, Deborah would like to offer you a free gift.

Simply go to the webpage below and remember to enter the gift code.

Please go to **www.DeborahPaiva.com/gift**

The gift code is: HEART

✌ NOTES ✌

❧ NOTES ❧

NOTES

NOTES

∿ NOTES ∿

NOTES

❧ NOTES ❧

∾ NOTES ∾

∾ NOTES ∾

∾ NOTES ∾

∾ NOTES ∾

NOTES

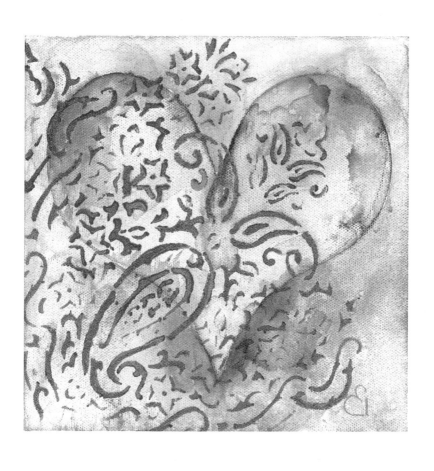